For my two nephews, who negotiated adolescence
successfully and have become fine adults.
– J. D.

For Wyatt, Owen, and Oscar:
May your road trip through adolescence be
filled with beautiful views and big adventures.
– T. D.

For Paul, whose love, creativity, optimism, and
support made this dedication a "no brainer."
– F. H.

Library of Congress Cataloging-in-Publication Data is available.
Library of Congress Control Number: 2013948836

ISBN 978-1-939775-02-3

13 12 11 10   1 2 3 4 5 6 7 8 9 10

Printed in the United States of America
First Edition 2013

Little Pickle Press, Inc.
3701 Sacramento Street #494
San Francisco, CA 94118

Please visit us at www.littlepicklepress.com.

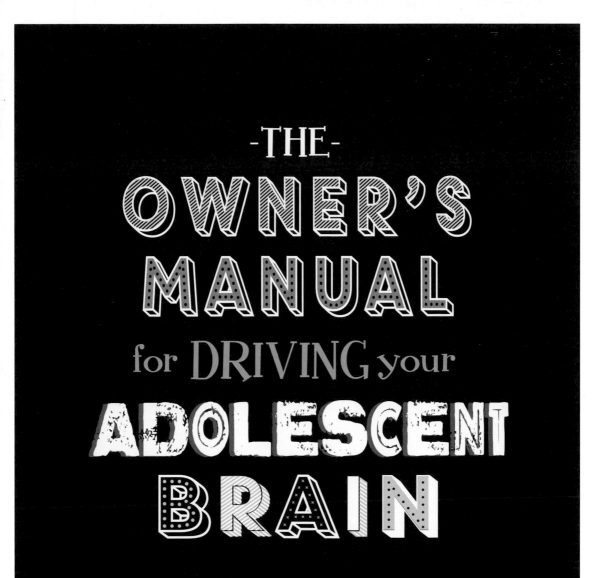

-THE-
OWNER'S MANUAL
for DRIVING your
ADOLESCENT
BRAIN

By JoAnn Deak, Ph.D. and
Terrence Deak, Ph.D.

Illustrated by Freya Harrison

Little Pickle Press

TABLE of CONTENTS

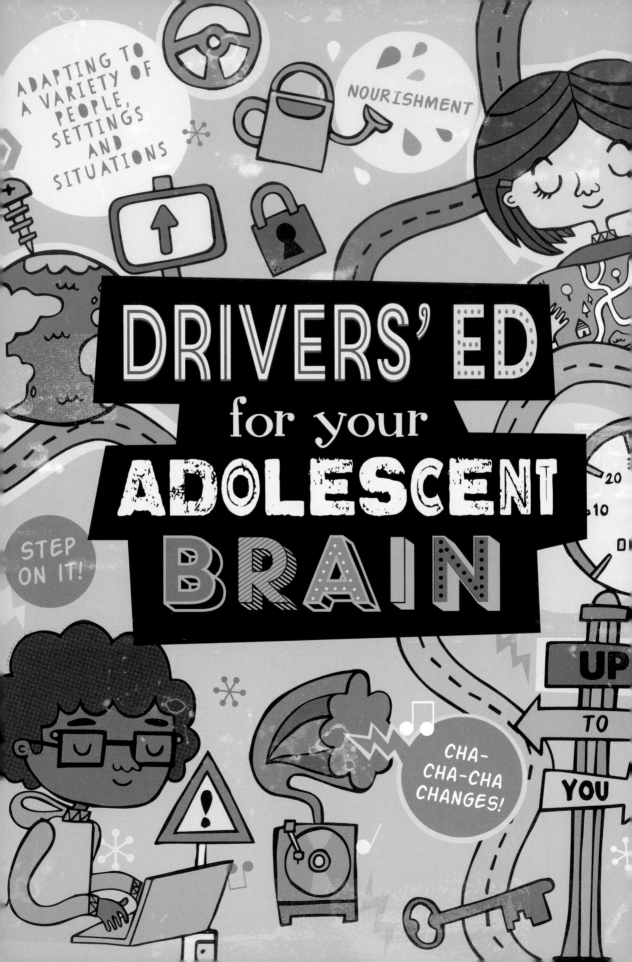

Have you ever sat in the driver's seat of your family car? It probably feels cool to press the pedals, honk the horn, and turn the wheel. But before you can drive that car, you'll have to learn a little more about how the car works (looking internally) and the rules for driving (looking externally) so that you can get where you want to go. To do this, you will learn practical driving tips from your parents, formal rules or laws from your teacher in a drivers' education class, and if you really want to be a great driver, you can learn how to maintain and protect your car by reading the owner's manual. Though not many people take the time to read these anymore, they are great little books—probably located in the glove box—that can help you interpret all of the warning signs on your dashboard and prevent problems down the road.

And just like learning to drive a car, learning about adolescence will help you deal with any bumps in the road. Does adolescence mean going on dates? Learning to drive? Trying to talk your parents into letting you stay out late? Yes, those are all likely to happen, but there is so much MORE going on in your brain! The pathway to your adult brain has not yet been paved and its final destination is not predetermined. As an adolescent, you have the amazing opportunity to blaze your own trail by shaping your brain, building its strengths, and avoiding dangers with the decisions you make. Your brain is a highly dynamic organ, and an amazing vehicle that will take you through many great life experiences. Wouldn't it be nice to have an owner's manual for your adolescent brain? Now you DO! This book will help you understand and appreciate YOUR brain. By knowing how it works, you can nurture and protect it in ways that will help you become the very best version of yourself!

Neuroscientists call the second decade of your life—from about age ten to age twenty—**adolescence**. Nearly all species—frogs, mice, birds, and even your beloved family dog or cat—go through this period of development. During this time, your brain, your body, your emotions, and even your interests change as you transform from a child into an adult. You will learn difficult things, such as why gravity affects everything in the universe. You will acquire complex skills like the ability to drive a car. And you will figure out how to adapt to a variety of people, settings, and situations. But it doesn't happen overnight. This is a complex transformation that will take about ten years to complete!

LET'S pop open the hood and LEARN

By the end of adolescence you may still have the same eye and hair color as the day you were born, but you will quite simply be a different person than you were before! What you do, think, and experience during this time will shape your brain and ultimately make you the unique person that you are meant to be. The most amazing part of all these changes is that **YOU** can have an impact on who you become by taking an interest in your brain. If you know a little more about the huge changes taking place, you will be better prepared to handle the challenges that you encounter during adolescence. You can train your brain to help you become the very best version of yourself!

a little about what makes this engine run!

In order to grow and thrive, your brain needs specific things. Above all, **time and experience** have the biggest impact. We all go through the stages of adolescence and brain development at about the same ages, and in about the same order. But the ticking clock alone is not enough to keep your brain growing. Your individual experiences can speed up or slow down these natural processes. And for your brain to reach its full potential, it needs three important ingredients:

- **NOURISHMENT**
- **ENRICHMENT**
- **PROTECTION**

BABY

Your brain is capable of only basic functions as an infant, such as lying under a play-gym and kicking your feet at the objects suspended above.

TODDLER

By two or three, you learn to pedal and can ride a tricycle.

CHILD

You quickly progress from training wheels to riding a bike independently.

TEEN

Your balance and abilities allow you to jump from ramps, ride on trails, and pay close attention to traffic.

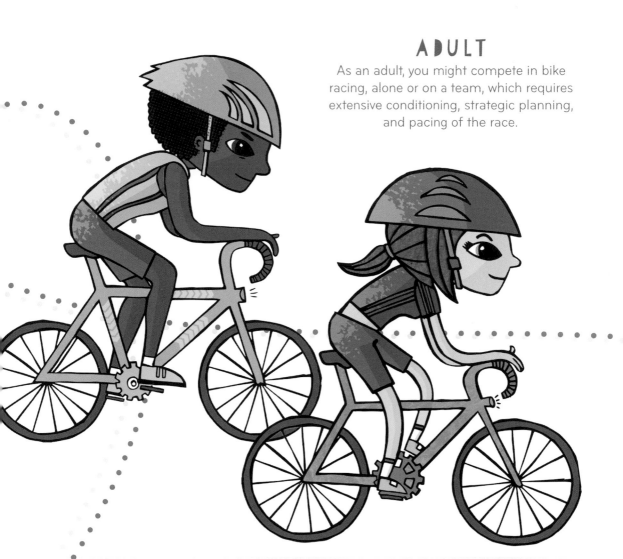

ADULT

As an adult, you might compete in bike racing, alone or on a team, which requires extensive conditioning, strategic planning, and pacing of the race.

Time + EXPERIENCE = GROWTH

When you put these essential elements together, your brain really starts revving! As an infant, your visual centers are one of the first things to develop as you begin to learn about your world. Around age four or five, your language centers begin to sound out words as you learn to read. During adolescence, your **corpus callosum**—the bridge between the left and right hemispheres of your brain—begins to thicken, making stronger connections between different parts of your brain, and suddenly things like abstract math start to click.

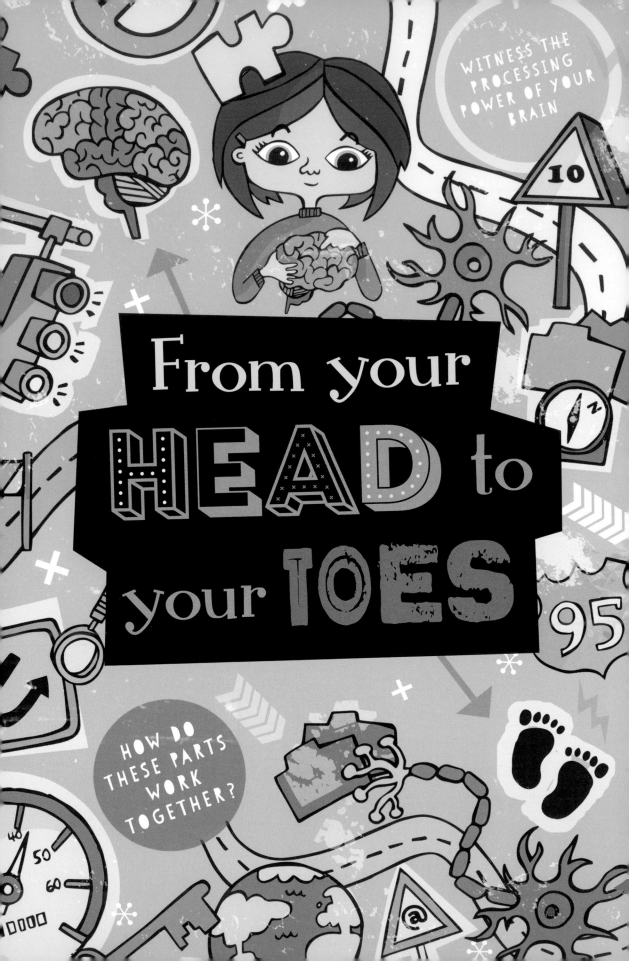

WITNESS THE PROCESSING POWER OF YOUR BRAIN

From your **HEAD** to your **TOES**

HOW DO THESE PARTS WORK TOGETHER?

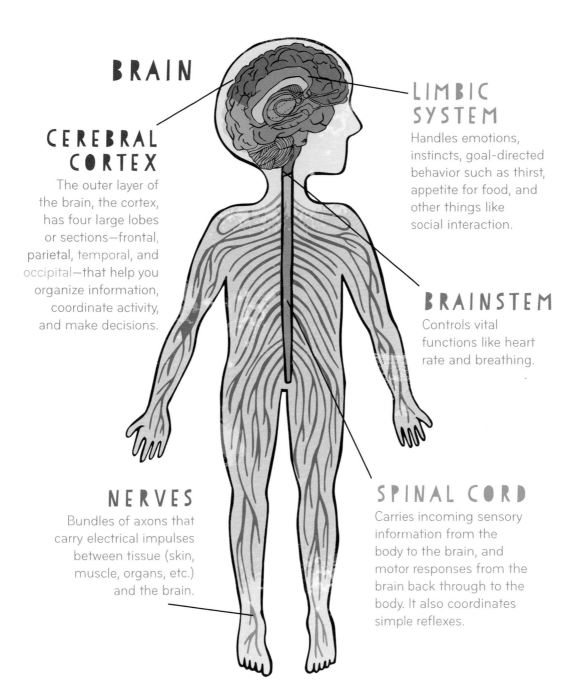

BRAIN

CEREBRAL CORTEX

The outer layer of the brain, the cortex, has four large lobes or sections—frontal, parietal, temporal, and occipital—that help you organize information, coordinate activity, and make decisions.

LIMBIC SYSTEM

Handles emotions, instincts, goal-directed behavior such as thirst, appetite for food, and other things like social interaction.

BRAINSTEM

Controls vital functions like heart rate and breathing.

NERVES

Bundles of axons that carry electrical impulses between tissue (skin, muscle, organs, etc.) and the brain.

SPINAL CORD

Carries incoming sensory information from the body to the brain, and motor responses from the brain back through to the body. It also coordinates simple reflexes.

Just as it's a good idea to learn all the essential parts of a car and how they work before you take it out for a spin, it is also important to understand how your brain is **organized** and how it **functions**. Your **central nervous system** is made up of the **brain** and **spinal cord**, which are inter-connected with nearly every other part of your body. Much like your digestive system has many specialized parts (stomach, small intestine, large intestine, etc.), your brain has many parts—or brain structures—that perform specific functions.

Inside your B-R-A-I-N

All of these brain structures are made up of **neurons**, which are the primary functional cells of the brain. Groups of neurons in one brain structure send their axons together to other brain structures, forming a **neural pathway**. Though most neurons follow a similar set of "rules" for how they operate, neurons come in slightly different styles and have slightly different abilities. What makes neurons unique from other cells in the body is that they are electrically charged like little batteries, and capable of processing electrical information like a teeny-tiny computer chip.

Think of the cell body as an iPod (capable of complex functions) and the axons as the wire to your ear buds (carries information to the speaker). Just think of the processing power when you put all 100 billion neurons in your brain together! But neurons can't do it alone—they require the support of other cells called **glia** (or glial cells). Glia provide nourishment for neurons by releasing proteins that act like fertilizer to help neurons grow and thrive. Glia also remove waste material and protect neurons from infection, damage, or other threats. Because of this, glia are very much like the mechanics at your local garage in the way they tend to neurons: Without an occasional oil change, wheel realignment, and full tank of gas, your car will break down, stall out, and leave you by the side of the road looking for help!

NEURON

MYELIN
A fatty substance produced by glia that surrounds axons, providing structural support and improved transmission of electrical impulses.

ASTROCYTE
(glial cell)

GLIA
Cells in the central nervous system that support, protect and nourish neurons.

AXON
This long branch extends from the cell body and carries signals to distant parts of your body.

OLIGODENDROCYTE
(glial cell)

DENDRITES
Bushy, branch-like structures that receive incoming signals from other neurons.

CELL BODY
Processes the information received from dendrites, and decides whether to send a message to another part of the brain.

When a neuron is activated it will release **neurotransmitters** from the end of its **axon** (or axon terminal) into the **synapse,** a very small space between the axon of one neuron and the dendrites or cell body of the next neuron. These neurotransmitters are tiny chemical messengers that cause electrical changes in nearby neurons by binding to receptors like a key fits into a lock. When a neurotransmitter binds to a receptor on a neuron, it will cause changes in that neuron that are specific to the type of neurotransmitter and the type of receptor to which it binds. There are two types of neurotransmitters: **Inhibitory neurotransmitters** send a **STOP** signal to the next neuron (like hitting the brakes) and **excitatory neurotransmitters** send a signal for the next neuron to **GO** (like stepping on the gas). Because every neuron receives thousands of chemical messages at the same time, each neuron is constantly "adding up" all of the STOP signals and GO signals so it can decide if it has received sufficient excitatory input to send electrical signals to the next neuron.

NEUROTRANSMITTERS

DID YOU KNOW ?

The axon from a single neuron can extend for as long as a meter! A single neuron in your spinal cord sends its axon all the way to the very tip of your toe to sense the environment and stimulate muscle contractions to provide balance while you walk. That is a **PRETTY AMAZING** feat for a cell body that is only about 100 microns in diameter (about the size of a pinhead). If the cell body were as big as a baseball, then its axon would extend nearly 2,416 feet! That is eight times as tall as the Statue of Liberty, twice as tall as the Eiffel Tower, and almost as high as the tallest skyscraper on Earth.

WHAT is Going On UP THERE?

So how do all these parts work together? Your brain's most important job is to help your body understand and interact with the world. To do this, your body has developed the sensory systems of taste, smell, touch, hearing, and vision. Would you believe that you don't actually see with your eyes alone, but with your brain?! Specialized sensory neurons translate messages from the environment into **electrical impulses**—the language of the brain. This is called **sensation**. In order for you to see an awesome sports car driving by, light particles called **photons** strike light-sensitive neurons in the back of your eye, causing those neurons to send electrical impulses to your brain. The primary visual cortex, inside the occipital lobe, receives these messages and then organizes them into a mental picture of what you see in front of you.

This process of organizing and decoding information that we take in through our senses is called **PERCEPTION.**

This is interpreted as a threat.
(Danger from car imminent!)

Your brain quickly detects
the loud sound (the horn).

Your brain engages evasive
maneuvers (Stepping backwards!)
within a few milliseconds
to protect you.

Sometimes we have to **act** on the information our brain receives very quickly. For instance, imagine that fancy sports car you saw is now speeding by just as you are about to cross the street, and the driver honks wildly at you. Now, watch as your brain springs into action!

It is pretty amazing when you realize how many things must happen inside your brain for you to make one little step. Your brain has to collect information from the world, decipher that information into a meaningful whole, and direct your body in ways that make sense, sometimes **saving your life**!

TEST your BRAIN POWER

TO WITNESS THE PROCESSING POWER OF YOUR BRAIN, TRY THIS EXPERIMENT.

AS A BUDDING YOUNG SCIENTIST, IT WOULD PROBABLY BE GOOD FOR YOU TO PERFORM THIS BLIND TASTE TEST WITH AS MANY FLAVORS OF ICE CREAM AS POSSIBLE.

CONVINCE YOUR PARENTS

to give you two bowls of different ice cream flavors
(strawberry and vanilla, for example).

Put on a blindfold and have someone put
a small spoonful in your mouth while you are

PLUGGING YOUR NOSE.

CAN YOU TELL WHICH FLAVOR
YOU ARE TASTING?

PROBABLY NOT.

This is because your taste system is only responsive to a few things—sweet, salty, bitter, sour, and savory. The rest of what we call "flavor" comes from your sense of smell (the **OLFACTORY** system). The delightful pleasure of strawberry ice cream is actually a combination of sweetness from the taste system PLUS strawberry odor from the olfactory system PLUS the physical sensation of the food on your tongue (smooth, cold, and creamy).

Your brain changes in size, structure, and ability throughout your childhood and adolescence. If you had a window into your head, you could easily see some significant changes: your brain gets larger and heavier overall, ridges (**gyri**) and folds (**sulci**) in the cortex (the outer layer of the brain) become more pronounced, and your brain takes on a more cauliflower-like shape.

But your brain doesn't just get bigger like a muscle or a bone—it gets way more complex and efficient in ways that are difficult to see (Especially without a microscope!). Pathways between neurons become stronger, structural changes make communication more efficient, and glia nourish and protect neurons more effectively.

Not all brain structures develop and mature at the same time or at the same rate. The **hindbrain** structures (the area at the back of your head), which regulate important functions like breathing and your heartbeat, are much more mature at birth than structures in the forebrain. The **forebrain** structures (closer to your forehead), like the cerebral cortex, which participates in complex decision-making and skills, are not fully developed until you are an adult.

BRING IT ON!

ADULTHOOD

To develop certain abilities like reading music or speaking a foreign language, you need to experience them at specific times in your life. These are called **critical periods**. For example, the critical period for learning a language is from birth through about age eight. If you hear sufficient spoken language during this time, the language centers in your brain will be better prepared for future language learning. Once the critical period has passed, the brain begins to **fossilize**. Once this happens you will still be able to learn a foreign language, but it will take a little more time and effort. You may be able to memorize vocabulary, but you may not be able to hear the fine sounds of the words or pronounce them like a native speaker.

MAKING MORE BRAIN

Did you know that your brain will continue to give birth to new neurons throughout your entire life? This process is called **NEUROGENESIS**. This happens mostly in brain structures that are important for **PLASTICITY**, or learning. You can supercharge your brain with regular exercise, which has been shown to increase neurogenesis!

Naked NEURONS

You were born with approximately 100 billion neurons, most of the neurons you will ever need. But many of them are short, skinny, and naked—and, like a baby bird that can't yet fly, immature. They are only capable of simple functions. You have the neurons you are going to use for more complex skills like reading later in life, but they didn't quite work when you were born. As you get older, they will become more robust, which means they get bigger, longer, and wider, until they reach their full size.

When the neurons are fully mature, the glial cells make a fatty, waxy substance called myelin, which wraps around the long axons. Just like the rubber that surrounds your ear bud wires, myelin protects the electrical signals from breaking up as they travel. This is especially important for neurons that send their axons long distances (like the one in your spinal cord that reaches to your toe). These long axons can be severed easily if they don't have protection. Without this myelin coat-

STAGES OF MYELINATION

As a newborn, very few axons in your brain are myelinated.

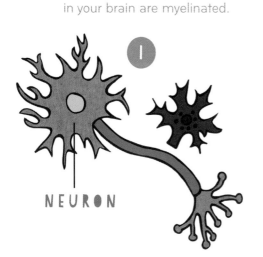

NEURON

OLIGODENDROCYTE
(glial cell)

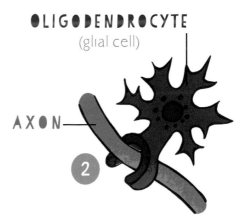

AXON

As you grow, myelin forms when glial cells extend their processes around an axon, much like your hand wrapping around the base of a bat.

ing, the output of those neurons becomes interrupted, just like when the sound that comes out of ear buds "crackles" and breaks up when there is a bad connection between your iPod and ear buds. Because neurons get coated with myelin (a process called **myelination**) throughout childhood, from birth through late adolescence, the impact of this process is revealed slowly over time. Different brain structures achieve their fully myelinated state at different ages, and as myelination becomes more extensive, the brain becomes more capable of complex skills.

Babies often make jerky movements as they reach toward their mother's nose, but by age two or three they are walking, running, and jumping, and their movements become smoother and more focused. As the brain continues to develop, you might start playing a sport like baseball. As a small child, you hit the ball off of a tee to learn how to swing at a stable target. Later, slow, underhand pitches from a coach help develop the timing of your swing. With some practice,

Glia encapsulate the axon by wrapping around it several times, producing a sheath that insulates and protects the electrical signals being transmitted.

Once myelination of the axon is complete, electrical signals are transmitted faster and more efficiently, enabling the development of skills and abilities that require faster processing power.

ONE

The visual system detects
the ball being pitched.

you will be capable of hitting faster, more difficult pitches from an automated pitching machine. Eventually, you will be ready to take on live pitchers who will test your abilities with sliders and knuckleballs at devilish speeds!

To hit a fast ball from a skilled pitcher, Your brain has to do a lot of work to knock one out of the park! First, you must be able to detect the ball being pitched, then coordinate a smooth muscular reaction involving the arms, trunk, and legs. At the same time, your brain must adjust the speed, height, and angle of the swing to hit the ball exactly where you want. And all of this happens within a fraction of a second!

Batting effectively is a carefully coordinated, complex skill that requires training of your brain. As you move into adolescence and take on more complex challenges (athletic or academic), remember that training your brain requires **patience** (you can't expect to be perfect your first time at bat), **practice** (skills need to be nurtured and systematically developed over time), and **persistence** (Don't give up!). After all, practice makes permanent—not perfect, as you might have heard!

TWO

Voluntary motor movements
(such as swinging the bat) are initiated
by the primary motor cortex.

THREE

Outgoing motor signals are adjusted by
the cerebellum, which refines rough signals
into smooth, coordinated action to make
contact with the ball.

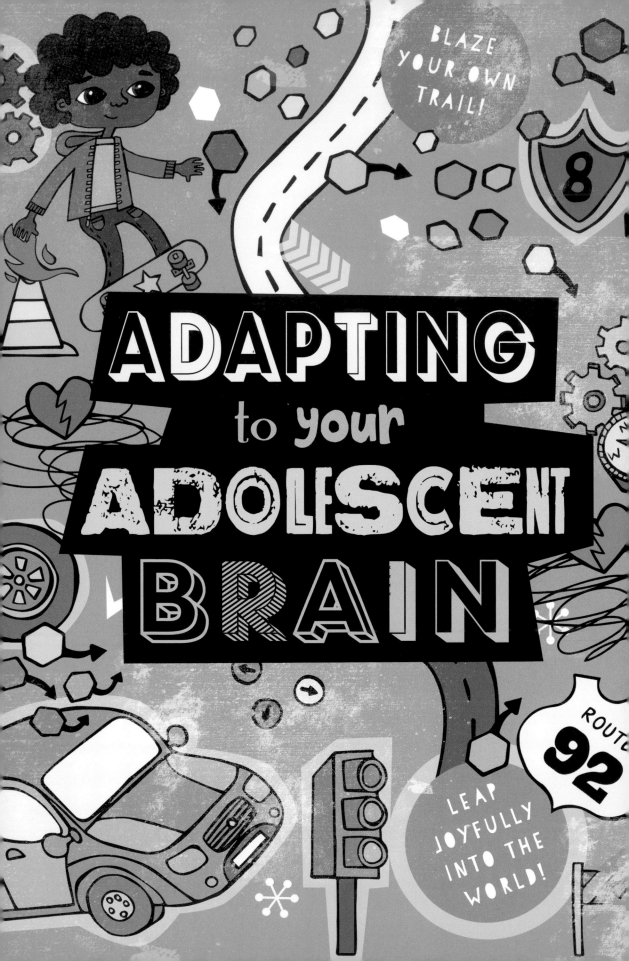

Up to this point we have talked about adolescence in general, which spans the entire developmental transition from childhood to adulthood. But puberty is its own distinct period during adolescence in which you will grow rapidly and your body becomes sexually mature. You have probably heard a lot about puberty and how your body goes through big changes as a teenager. But did you know that puberty starts in your brain? It's true! Just prior to puberty, a small group of neurons in the **hypothalamus** (a structure toward the very bottom of your brain) begin to produce a protein called **kisspeptin**. Because the number of kisspeptin neurons in your brain have been increasing as you age, there will eventually be enough kisspeptin to stimulate the release of a specific hormone called **gonadotropin-releasing hormone (GnRH)**, which then stimulates the release of **testosterone** (in males) and **estrogen** (in females). Hormones are chemicals released from glands into your blood, which then travel around and have widespread effects throughout your brain and body. When exactly will this happen to you? The truth is that while we all go through puberty, we don't all go through it at the same age. Some people experience puberty around as early as eight or nine years old, while others don't experience puberty until they are well into high school.

CHANGES IN YOUR BODY START WITH CHANGES IN YOUR BRAIN

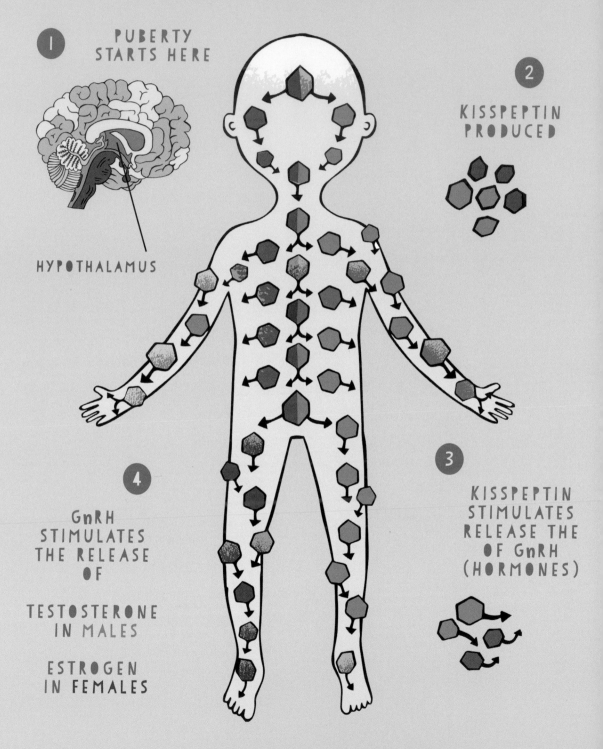

1 PUBERTY STARTS HERE

HYPOTHALAMUS

2 KISSPEPTIN PRODUCED

3 KISSPEPTIN STIMULATES RELEASE THE OF GnRH (HORMONES)

4 GnRH STIMULATES THE RELEASE OF

TESTOSTERONE IN MALES

ESTROGEN IN FEMALES

HORMONES SURGE AROUND BODY

Remember, this is a natural process
in your brain and you
CAN'T CONTROL IT.

So far, your relationship with your body and with other people has probably been like riding a tricycle—you get where you want to go at a safe and slow pace. But once you hit puberty, the hormonal surge is like driving a car for the first time: You can go a whole lot faster, and do a little fish-tailing, but sometimes you might lose control and spin out. No matter how careful you think you are being, you simply don't quite know how to drive a race car **YET**!

HORMONES shape your BODY

The first thing you will probably notice when you start puberty are the physical changes that are caused by hormones. Boys and girls have different hormones that help them develop in sex-specific ways. Boys undergo a surge in testosterone released from their testes, whereas girls have a surge in estrogen hormones from their ovaries. These hormones cause changes such as increased hair production in the genital (and other) areas, breast development in girls, deepening of the voice for boys, and many other changes that make you look more like an adult. In addition to these physical changes, the timing of puberty onset also differs between boys and girls. For instance, because girls tend to experience puberty earlier than boys, their behavior often transforms from friendliness to romance long before boys are ready. This is why you can often find girls chasing boys around the playground for a kiss, and not the other way around!

Making Mental Maps

Just as your body is transformed during puberty by hormonal and chemical chang-es, your interactions with others and the world around you are also affected by this chemistry. For nearly all species, adolescence is a transitional period that ultimately prepares the individual to "leave the nest." While you will still want to hang out with your old friends, you may start to become interested in new and different activities. The rational part of your brain is growing, and playing with action figures or dressing up for imaginary tea parties may start to seem less excit-ing than going on big adventures. Early on, rough-and-tumble play and "wres-tling around" was hard-wired in deep structures of your brain as an important way of learning. But as an adolescent, structured activities or complex computer games will likely be more appealing to your growing cortex. And instead of play-ing in the backyard, you will be compelled by changes in the limbic system to do more exploring, which will ultimately help you form a "mental map" of your com-munity. You will be discovering more about your environment and experiencing many new things, so that when the time comes, you are prepared to leave the family nest and leap joyfully into the world.

BRING ON the DRAMA

As you grow into your teenage years, your feelings, thoughts, and relationships will also start to change. Some friendships will become stronger, while you may also find new friends who share your growing obsessions with soccer, indie music, or fashion design. This period of intense friendships and relationships is both exciting and difficult, and is a natural result of changes happening in your brain during adolescence. Most notably, however, you will start to have romantic feelings. The intensity of these feelings will be greater than you can imagine. Like the changes in your body, these romantic feelings and attractions are probably intensified by your surging hormones, which seem to "turn up the volume" on natural aspects of adolescent brain development. To put it simply, your body is preparing for adult social interactions and relationships, and ultimately, reproduction. And remember, even if you feel overwhelmed by the intensity of your emotions at times, this is **normal**, and it won't last forever.

FIND YOUR NORTH STAR

At some point you are probably going to be heartbroken by a crush, wounded by a so-called friend, or bashed by a bully. It might even happen all on the same day, making you feel like you are being pulled in ten different directions at once. But scientists have discovered that pursuing important passions like music, sports, or writing can hold you steady when you feel overwhelmed. This is sometimes referred to as a North Star, a point of light in the darkness to guide you. If you are passionate about horseback riding, visit your local barn and spend some time grooming your favorite horse. Or if you dream of performing in your own band, find some quiet time to practice your guitar. Staying true to what matters to YOU can go a long way toward relieving painful experiences and stress.

IF YOU SNOOZE YOU ... WIN!

Sleep is one of the greatest mysteries of the human brain. Scientists have learned many things about how we fall asleep and how sleep is controlled by our brains, but we still know very little about how sleep reenergizes our brains and impacts our mood. What we do know is that daily activities and long-term development of the brain are **seriously** impacted if we don't get enough sleep.

It is not unusual for teenagers to feel as if they can't get enough sleep, especially in the morning. But teens aren't simply lazy. In fact, this is caused by a change in **melatonin**, a hormone that makes you drowsy. During puberty, melatonin is released from the pineal gland much later in the day than in young children, so adolescents often have difficulty falling asleep. It is a bit like a natural form of "jetlag," though it occurs as a natural part of puberty rather than from crossing time zones! However, teens still need as much as nine hours of sleep per night to function properly the next day and give their brains sufficient time to grow, change, and reenergize during sleep. So why should you care about how sleep patterns shift during adolescence? Scientists have uncovered amazing evidence that what your brain learns during the day is **consolidated** during sleep. That means the more sleep you get, the better your brain will remember and understand what you learned that day.

PAYING BACK YOUR SLEEP DEBT

At certain times during adolescence you might develop what is called a "sleep debt" from staying up later but still getting up early for school! Your brain "pays back" this sleep debt on the weekends, and you might sleep for a very long time. Sleeping late on weekends to pay back that sleep debt is a natural—and necessary—process. Because sleeping late is often a source of conflict between adolescents and their parents—who would prefer that the chores get done and commitments to ballet, baseball, or playing the bassoon are kept—some careful planning of your weekly activities to prevent going too far into debt may may help relieve some conflict.

Maintain a smorgasbord attitude

Although you may feel compelled to spend every waking minute practicing show tunes for chorus or mastering your new video game, adolescence is a good time to sample new experiences and expand your borders. Learning a new sport, discovering a new place to explore, and expanding your circle of friends are all healthy ways to engage your brain. The more you stimulate, challenge, and stretch your mind, the more **neurotrophins** your brain will produce. Neurotrophins are proteins produced by glial cells that act like fertilizer for your brain, stimulating neurogenesis and increasing your brain power! The result is that your brain will be more resilient during times of stress, more capable of handling new experiences, and more likely to reach its greatest potential!

THE POWER OF PROTECTION

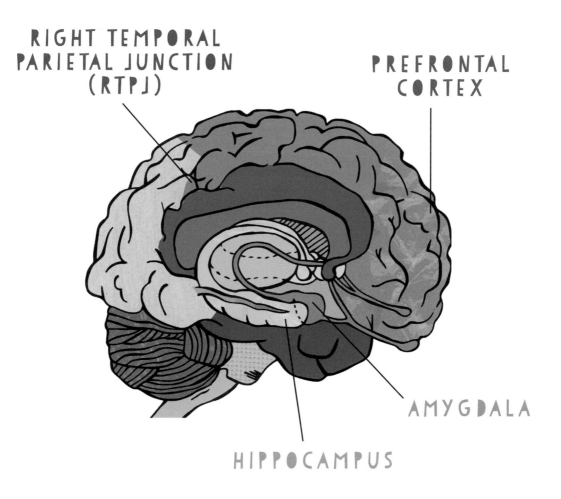

RIGHT TEMPORAL PARIETAL JUNCTION (RTPJ)

PREFRONTAL CORTEX

AMYGDALA

HIPPOCAMPUS

Since the day you were born, two important parts of your brain—the **amygdala** and the **hippocampus**—have worked automatically, like a programmed computer, to keep you out of harm's way. The amygdala becomes activated when you feel a very strong emotion—especially in response to a fearful situation—and files that intense emotion in your memory bank. The hippocampus, on the other hand, helps you remember people, places, and events associated with a particular memory. So if you are bitten by a snake, your amygdala ensures that you remain fearful of snakes in the future and the hippocampus makes certain that you remember the location where it happened. Working together, connections between your amygdala and hippocampus ensure that other important environmental cues (small crevices in rocks or burrows in the dirt; the hiss or rattle of a snake) are used to predict where snakes might be lying in wait and effectively protect you from future bites.

PROTECT yourself and others

It is easy to imagine the pain of a hammer slamming onto your thumb or your first love breaking up with you. But it takes **empathy** to allow you to recognize how someone else feels. This is different from **sympathy**, which is simply your own personal emotion about the experiences of others. Scientists believe that one brain structure—the **right temporal parietal junction (RTPJ)**—is particularly important for developing empathy, a critical ingredient for positive social interactions throughout life. To understand where the RTPJ is located, place your finger an inch above your right ear, and then move it an inch toward the back of your head. Buried under your skull and nestled in your brain tissue is this specialized region that devotes itself to a very important task: understanding other people.

Empathy is an essential function
that makes us
UNIQUELY HUMAN.

with EMPATHY and INTERACTION

It is especially important to be aware of how you use your RTPJ in today's high-tech world. Recent data suggests that many young people may not be using their RTPJ as much as they could because they spend so much time communicating electronically through digital devices, text messages, or social networks. While scientists are still figuring out how relationships built through technology compare to personal interaction, most believe that person-to-person connection is essential for adolescents to learn effective and appropriate ways of interacting in the world. This is true in other species as well: when contact with other rodents is restricted, even these small creatures fail to develop normal social interactions. These effects are particularly pronounced when social interaction is restricted during adolescence, suggesting that this is a critical/sensitive period for social interaction. You can improve your own chances for healthy social interaction as an adult by ensuring that your interactions with others are not limited to just electronic means such as texting or e-mailing.

EXPERIENCE EMOTION

One of the keys to the growth of the RTPJ (in addition to a lot of use) is connecting experiences with the emotional part of the brain. Which of these two examples do you think most effectively strengthens the RTPJ?

A.
You throw a can of sweet potatoes into the box that will be given to families without enough food for Thanksgiving.

B.
You spend a day working in a soup kitchen that serves homeless families.

Answer: (B) In the same way that the smell of turkey on Thanksgiving Day reminds you of your grandparents, cousins, and family traditions, combining complex sensory experiences (sights, sounds, and smells) with the emotional experience of interacting with others helps you develop a richer understanding of other people. If you work on developing empathy for others now, you will be more likely to have positive relationships and interactions with your friends, family, and other people you meet in your teen years and beyond!

STICKS & STONES

The RTPJ is not the only brain structure involved with empathy and other aspects of social interaction. When it comes to the brain, emotional pain (like the kind you feel when you're teased) is very similar to physical pain (like getting stung by a bee). In a clever study several years ago, researchers watched the brains of people who were asked to play a game with a "friendly" computer. After a while, the computer announced that it did not want to play anymore, causing the person to feel socially rejected. The researchers found that even the minor pain of being rejected by a computer (not even a person!) activated the **anterior cingulate cortex (ACC)**, the same part of the brain that is activated when you slam your finger in the door or scrape your knee. These findings tell us two important things. First, your brain has one neural pathway that translates both physical and psychological pain, and second, that social rejection is truly painful! The next time you are tempted to tease someone in the locker room or exclude a new kid from the lunch table, think about how you might take more positive action instead. Not only could you make someone's day, you will also be strengthening your RTPJ and empowering your brain!

DO YOUR BRAIN A FAVOR

This book would not be complete without talking about a few things that can threaten your brain development during adolescence. Your brain has a special pathway called the **mesolimbic dopamine system**, which is made of connections between the **ventral tegmental area** and the **nucleus accumbens**. Normally, this neural pathway is activated by natural rewards such as social interaction, tasty food, and sexual activity (among other things). When you consume alcohol or other drugs, this pathway becomes even more activated, causing you to seek out those substances over and over again. Over time, this behavior can become more pathological and ultimately result in addiction. When a person becomes addicted to alcohol or other drugs, the addiction can "hijack" other priorities like commitments to work, school, family, and friends, leading to serious consequences.

Drinking alcohol would have a very different effect on you than it does on your parents because your brain is still developing. Alcohol isn't just unhealthy for the neurons you have—it also reduces neurogenesis, the ability of your brain to grow new neurons, and ultimately reduces how much you can learn later in life. Adolescents metabolize, or process, alcohol through their bodies faster than adults. Because of this, they often consume more and are less sensitive to "hangover" effects. Adolescents even show fewer signs of intoxication, like a staggered walk or sleepiness, than adults who have the same blood alcohol levels might. All of these subtle differences together create the "perfect storm" for alcohol abuse. Though not everyone who has an occasional drink will develop into an alcoholic, it is clear that the younger you start to drink, the higher your risk of becoming an alcoholic down the road. This probably occurs, at least in part, because you would have "trained" your brain to be highly "successful" at consuming alcohol later in life.

Alcohol and other drugs are not the only threat to your developing brain. Your brain is also susceptible to damage caused by **INJURY**.

Even though your brain is encased within the hard bones of your skull, its soft tissue can still be seriously damaged if you are hit in the head, as with a concussion. To understand how this can happen, put a marble inside a travel mug and shake it back and forth. That noise you hear is the marble banging the inside walls of the mug. Now take the marble out, put a peeled grape inside the mug, and shake it vigorously. You might find that the peeled grape (approximately the same consistency of your brain) is bent out of shape and leaking its juices. This is what happens when you fall from your bike and hit your head on the curb, bang your head on the ground as you are tackled during a football game, or fall from the balance beam in gymnastics class. To avoid turning your brain into grape jelly, take advantage of the many safety measures that have been developed to help protect your brain. Wearing helmets and soft pads will protect the "gear" inside your head, ensuring that you can enjoy that activity for many years to come.

PROTECT IT BACK!

NOBODY said it

The **prefrontal cortex**, or PFC, is known as the "executive" part of the brain—like the President of the United States, or the head of a large company. The PFC is critical for your planning and decision-making, which are defining characteristics of a fully mature, adult brain. The PFC matures significantly during your teen years, and scientists are learning more every day about how it works. Even if you want to make all the right choices to take care of your brain—being kind to yourself, avoiding drugs and alcohol, and learning to help others—you may find that you make more mistakes than not. Recent research has shown that adolescents often act impulsively or engage in risky behaviors in part because the PFC is not yet fully mature, and not yet capable of effectively reigning in impulsive actions. This may be because adolescents don't have as much GABA, a key inhibitory neurotransmitter, in their PFC as adults. Because of this, the adolescent PFC is probably a little extra "excitable," leading to teens being more impulsive than adults, who are better able to control their behavior.

would be easy

And while it can seem impossible to avoid all the pitfalls of adolescence when they are in your face every day, you can make it easier to protect yourself, your friends, and your brain. When something is important, STOP, then take a moment to let your PFC study and evaluate the situation before taking action. And while your friends are no doubt awesome at picking out new shoes at the mall or coming up with the best party playlist ever, sometimes YOU know what is best for yourself. By making important decisions on your own instead of relying only on your friends, you can strengthen your PFC and help it achieve its full potential. And, even if it isn't easy, you might ask the advice of a trusted adult, who has a fully robust PFC. Understanding the adult perspective will help your adolescent PFC function more like an adult PFC.

The choice is yours . . .
WHICH WAY will you go?

To finally reach its full potential, your brain needs to gain strength. Some of this strength will come naturally as you grow and take care of your body. But you can also be proactive by enriching your brain with a combination of physical and mental exercises, strengthening its powers and sharpening its focus.

TIME for A

During the first ten years of your life, your brain went through a time of extensive growth known as **proliferation**. This is especially noticeable in dendrites, the ends of neurons which look like the limbs of a tree. The more your brain makes connections in the world, the more these dendrites grow (a process called **arborization** from the Latin word arbor, which means "tree"). You can grow thousands of dendrites for every neuron, making them look like a wild and sprawling bush in your backyard.

Once you become an adolescent, this kind of development and growth changes course and instead of growing like a wild weed, your brain begins **pruning**. Just like pruning a bush, brain areas like the amygdala, prefrontal cortex, and nucleus accumbens will now start to be cut back. This means

Your brain is strengthening the neural pathways that get used **THE MOST**.

LITTLE GARDENING

that your brain is strengthening the neural pathways that get used the most. Scientists often say that "neurons that fire together wire together." For instance, if you practice the piano every day, the skills you use to play become "hardwired" into the structure and function of the brain.

However, pathways in your brain that are not used as much will ultimately wither away, much like a flower that doesn't get watered enough. If math is your least favorite subject and you stop taking math classes, those parts of your brain that deal with math will weaken, and math will continue to be hard for you. But if you keep plugging ahead, even if you don't quite "get it," you will strengthen your brain and that strength will remain for your entire life. Another good reason to keep at that algebra homework is that learning math also enhances parts of your brain that do many other complex tasks every day—like playing your favorite Mozart tune on the piano—with the added benefit that you also develop those math skills!

STRUGGLE makes you STRONGER

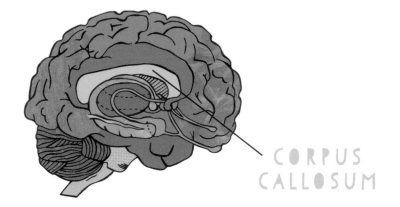

CORPUS
CALLOSUM

Another part of your brain that is under major construction during adolescence is the **corpus callosum**. This is a thick band of nerve tissue that acts as the bridge between the left and right hemispheres of the brain. The corpus callosum is largely made of axon fibers originating from neurons in other brain structures. As a younger child, your corpus callosum is not yet completely formed. If you take music lessons, your brain is capable of only basic elements such as rhythm (clapping in time), pitch (singing simple songs), and motion (dancing). As the axons become myelinated, they are able to communicate with other neurons even faster and more accurately so that you are able to progress to more complex skills like reading music and playing an instrument.

Once you reach adolescence and your corpus callosum has become more developed, you can move on to more complex skills like learning to play the guitar. Here, your eyes will need to track notes on the musical staff (a form of reading using a totally different alphabet), convert those notes to precise movements of your fingers as they press the correct fret, and perfectly time the motion of your other hand as it picks and strums the strings. Don't forget about your foot, which is probably tapping on the floor like a metronome to keep the time, and your ears, which monitor the sound in real time and allow you to make subtle adjustments to improve the quality of the notes being played. To do all of this, your brain will have to have excellent communication between many brain structures, and it will have to happen fast!

Your corpus callosum plays a key role in all of this. Think of the corpus callosum as a multilane highway that bridges two parts of a major city. You will need as strong a bridge as possible to use on a daily basis throughout life. This is the time to set a sturdy foundation by engaging in complex thinking, learning new things, and attempting difficult tasks.

IT'S OK TO MAKE MISTAKES

The corpus callosum and the PFC work together, as do many other structures of the brain. But making mistakes occurs frequently when learning more complicated skills that require multiple parts of the brain. This is good! Newer research is showing that making mistakes actually enhances the function of the PFC and corpus callosum. When you have to struggle, think, figure out what to do next, fail, and try again, you are giving these parts a good workout and strengthening the neural pathways necessary to get the job done right. Don't wait until you have the right answer or just do what is easy. It's okay to make mistakes—they will make you stronger, if you use them as an opportunity to learn!

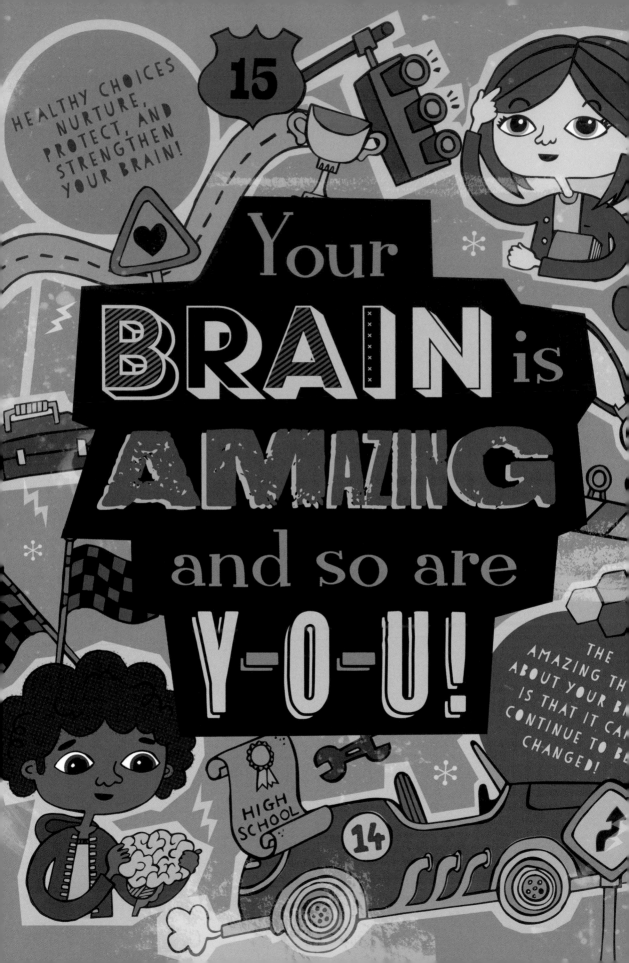

As you can see, your brain and body are about to pass through a dynamic period of development that will drive you toward many new and exciting adventures as an adolescent. Some of these changes will jump out at you like a deer crossing the highway, and other times you will be able to steer carefully around the obstacles in your path. As you embark upon these adventures, be sure to occasionally consult your owner's manual to better understand what's going on under the hood, and perform some general maintenance to ensure your engine continues to run smoothly.

You might be concerned that you have missed an opportunity to grow your brain, or that you made some wrong choices. Forget about it! The amazing thing about your brain is that—particularly in the first two decades of life—it can still be changed! It might take a little extra practice to re-wire some of the ways your brain has been shaped by your experiences, but just like the guitarist who learned a wrong riff, with the right attitude, some conviction toward change, and a little bit of practice, you too can learn a new "riff" for your brain! If you want to shape your adolescent brain in powerfully positive ways, then embracing your growing independence with positive, healthy choices that nurture, protect, and strengthen your brain will set the stage for a brighter future. There are thousands of scientists around the world working to understand how your brain works. That means two important things: First, there is a ton of information available about your brain—**go explore it!** And second, there are many mysteries of the brain that have yet to be solved—**go explore them!**

GLOSSARY

ADOLESCENCE

The developmental period (usually from about age ten to age twenty) during which your brain and body transform from child to adult.

AMYGDALA

A part of the limbic system involved in a range of emotional processes and emotional learning, especially fear and anxiety. The amygdala is also an important brain site for regulation of social interaction and aggression.

ANTERIOR CINGULATE CORTEX

A specialized portion of the frontal cortex that deals with rational thinking, decision-making, empathy, impulse control, and the experience of emotions.

ARBORIZATION

A term used to describe the amount of dendritic branching on a neuron. Dendritic arborization changes dynamically across brain development and in response to life experiences.

AXON

Projections extending from neurons that transmit electrical impulses to the next neuron(s) in series.

AXON TERMINAL

The very end of an axon from which a neurotransmitter is released into the synapse.

BRAINSTEM

A general term used to describe the structures at the base of the brain (including the medulla and pons) involved in vital functions such as heart rate, blood pressure, and respiration.

CEREBELLUM

A large structure in the back part of the brain that helps to refine, smooth, and coordinate motor movements.

CORPUS CALLOSUM

A wide bundle of nerve fibers that connects the two hemispheres of the brain.

CEREBRAL CORTEX

The outer layer of the brain that deals with decision-making, attention, language processing, and many other functions associated with consciousness.

DENDRITE

Branched projections of neurons which receive incoming electrochemical signals from other neurons.

ESTROGENS

A family of hormones released by the ovaries in females that cause the development of secondary sex characteristics (breast development, hair growth, etc) in females. Estrogen is also present in males, though in lesser quantities than in females.

FOREBRAIN

The anterior (front) portions of the brain, including the cerebral cortex, thalamus, and hypothalamus.

GABA

An acronym for gamma-aminobutyric acid. This is one of the most prevalent inhibitory neurotransmitters in your brain.

GLIA

Cells in the brain and spinal cord that provide support for neurons by clearing waste generated by neurons, releasing substances that support healthy neurons, and providing structural support (via the myelin sheath) to axons.

GnRH (gonadotropin releasing hormone)

A hormone released by the pituitary gland that stimulates the gonads (testes in males, ovaries in females) to release sex-specific hormones (testosterone in males, estrogen in females).

GYRUS OR GYRI

A ridge or ridges in the cerebral cortex. Gyri are surrounded by sulci, or folds, in the cerebral cortex.

HINDBRAIN

The back part of the brain, including the brainstem (medulla and pons) and the cerebellum.

HIPPOCAMPUS

A part of the limbic system involved with many aspects of learning and memory, including acquisition of new knowledge, consolidation, and retrieval of memories. The hippocampus is particularly important in forming mental maps (or spatial learning).

HORMONES

Substances released from the brain and endocrine glands into the blood stream that impact cells in distant parts of the body.

HYPOTHALAMUS

An area at the base of the brain just below the thalamus that deals with goal-directed behavior (appetite for food and specific nutrients, thirst, sexual and social behavior) and coordination of endocrine function (hormone release).

KISSPEPTIN

A small peptide (or protein) in the hypothalamus that is important for the initiation of puberty.

LIMBIC SYSTEM

A group of brain structures involved with emotion, motivation, and learning and memory processes.

MELATONIN

A hormone released by the pineal gland. Melatonin secretion varies throughout the day and helps coordinate daily biological rhythms, including the sleep-wake cycle.

MESOLIMBIC DOPAMINE SYSTEM

A specialized neural system involved in the experience of pleasure.

MYELIN

A fatty substance lining the axons of neurons that provides structural support and speeds up electrical transmission of neural impulses. Myelin is produced by glia.

MYELINATION

The process by which myelin develops in the nervous system. Myelination is one of the last components of brain development to be completed during late adolescence and early adulthood and plays an important role in strengthening neuronal communication by improving the speed and protecting electrical signals carried by axons.

NEURAL PATHWAY

A collection of axon fibers that connect one cluster of neurons (or brain structure) to another.

NEUROGENESIS

The process by which new neurons are "born" in the brain.

NEURON

Specialized cells in your brain that send and receive information by transmitting electrical impulses.

NEUROSCIENTIST

Individual who studies the brain as a career.

NEUROTRANSMITTERS

Substances released from neurons that serve as chemical messengers to other neurons and cells.

OCCIPITAL LOBE

The very back part of the cerebral cortex, which includes the primary visual cortex and other structures.

PLASTICITY

Changes in neural function that occur as a result of experience.

PREFRONTAL CORTEX

A specialized area of the frontal cortex that is involved in executive function (decision-making, planning, and problem-solving).

PRIMARY VISUAL CORTEX

An area of the cerebral cortex, in the back of the brain, that is responsible for assembling information received by the eyes (retina) into mental images.

PROLIFERATION

The process of cells dividing and increasing in number.

PUBERTY

A period of development when sexual maturation occurs. Puberty is controlled by the brain, which induces a surge in pubertal hormones from the gonads (ovaries in females; testes in males).

RECEPTORS

Proteins that bind to neurotransmitters and cause changes in cells.

ROBUST

A term used to describe neurons that have achieved full functionality.

SENSORY NEURONS

Specialized neurons that convert stimuli from the environment into neural impulses.

SULCUS OR SULCI

The inner folds of the cerebral cortex. Sulci are surrounded by gyri.

SYNAPSE

A small space at the junction between two neurons. Most synapses sit between the axon terminal of one neuron and the dendrite of another neuron, though some synapses also occur between axons and cell bodies. This is where neurotransmitter is released.

TESTOSTERONE

A hormone released by the testes in males that causes the development of secondary sex characteristics (hair and muscular growth, deepening of voice, etc) during puberty. Females also make testosterone, though in lesser quantities than males.

For MORE INFORMATION

If you would like to learn more about your brain and how it works, you may want to explore the research of Dr. Jay Geidd of the Child Psychiatry Branch of the National Institute of Mental Health (www.nimh.nih.gov/media/video/giedd.shtml). His images of the insides of teen brains will blow your mind!

The Dana Foundation, a private philanthropic organization, supports brain research through grants and educates the public about the successes and potential of brain research (www.dana.org).

The Primal Teen by Barbara Strauch is written for adults, but offers a great deal of valuable information on scientific discoveries about the changes the brain goes through during adolescence that would be of interest to all ages.

INDEX

Our Mission

Little Pickle Press is dedicated to helping parents and educators cultivate conscious, responsible little people by stimulating explorations of the meaningful topics of their generation through a variety of media, technologies, and techniques.

Little Pickle Press
Environmental Benefits Statement

This book is printed on Appleton Utopia U2:XG Extra Green Paper. It is made with 30% PCRF (Post-Consumer Recovered Fiber) and Green Power. It is FSC®-certified, acid-free, and ECF (Elemental Chlorine-Free). All of the electricity required to manufacture the paper used to print this book is matched with RECS (Renewable Energy Credits) from Green-e® certified energy sources, primarily wind.

Little Pickle Press saved the following resources by using U2:XG paper:

trees	energy	greenhouse gases	wastewater	solid waste
Post-consumer recovered fiber displaces wood fiber with savings translated as trees.	PCRF content displaces energy used to process equivalent virgin fiber.	Measured in CO_2 equivalents, PCRF content and Green Power reduce greenhouse gas emissions.	PCRF content eliminates wastewater needed to process equivalent virgin fiber.	PCRF content eliminates solid waste generated by producing an equivalent amount of virgin fiber through the pulp and paper manufacturing process.
19 trees	**9 mil BTUs**	**1,624 lbs**	**8,811 gal**	**590 lbs**

Calculations based on research by Environmental Defense Fund and other members of the Paper Task Force and applies to print quanities of 7,500 books.

B Corporations are a new type of company that use the power of business to solve social and environmental problems. Little Pickle Press is proud to be a Certified B Corporation.

ABOUT the AUTHORS

JOANN DEAK, PH.D., is an author and an international speaker, educator, and preventive psychologist. She also works with parents, teachers, and other adults who work with children as a consultant to schools worldwide on issues of brain development and gender equality. She is also the author of the award-winning book, *Your Fantastic Elastic Brain*.

TERRENCE DEAK, PH.D. is a Professor of Psychology and Behavioral Neuroscience at Binghamton University in upstate New York, where he runs a highly active neuroscience laboratory. Dr. Deak and his wife, Molly, have 3 inquisitive boys (Wyatt, Owen, and Oscar) who are extremely interested in how their brains work, just like you. Together, they enjoy a plethora of outdoor activities, travel, and learning something new every day.

ABOUT the ILLUSTRATOR

FREYA HARRISON began drawing as soon as she could hold a pencil (so her mum says). Since then she's graduated with a B.A. in Graphic and Media Design from University of the Arts, London and has been doodling pictures for books, magazines, festivals, and brands ever since. She works and lives in London amongst a small mountain of comics, records, and sharpies. Find Freya's work on the web at www.freyaillustration.co.uk.

OTHER AWARD-WINNING BOOKS FROM LITTLE PICKLE PRESS

THE COW IN PATRICK O'SHANAHAN'S KITCHEN

Written by Diana Prichard   Illustrated by Heather Devlin Knopf

SPAGHETTI IS NOT A FINGER FOOD (AND OTHER LIFE LESSONS)

Written by Jodi Carmichael   Illustrated by Sarah Ackerley

BIG

Written by Coleen Paratore   Illustrated by Clare Fennell

RIPPLE'S EFFECT

Written by Shawn Achor and Amy Blankson   Illustrated by Cecilia Rebora

SNUTT THE IFT: A SMALL BUT SIGNIFICANT CHAPTER IN THE LIFE OF THE UNIVERSE

Written and Illustrated by Helen Ward

YOUR FANTASTIC ELASTIC BRAIN: STRETCH IT, SHAPE IT

Written by JoAnn Deak, Ph.D.   Illustrated by Sarah Ackerley

SOFIA'S DREAM

Written by Land Wilson   Illustrated by Sue Cornelison

WHAT DOES IT MEAN TO BE SAFE?

Written by Rana DiOrio   Illustrated by Sandra Salsbury

WHAT DOES IT MEAN TO BE PRESENT?

Written by Rana DiOrio   Illustrated by Eliza Wheeler

WHAT DOES IT MEAN TO BE GREEN?

Written by Rana DiOrio   Illustrated by Chris Blair

WHAT DOES IT MEAN TO BE GLOBAL?

Written by Rana DiOrio   Illustrated by Chris Hill

WWW.LITTLEPICKLEPRESS.COM

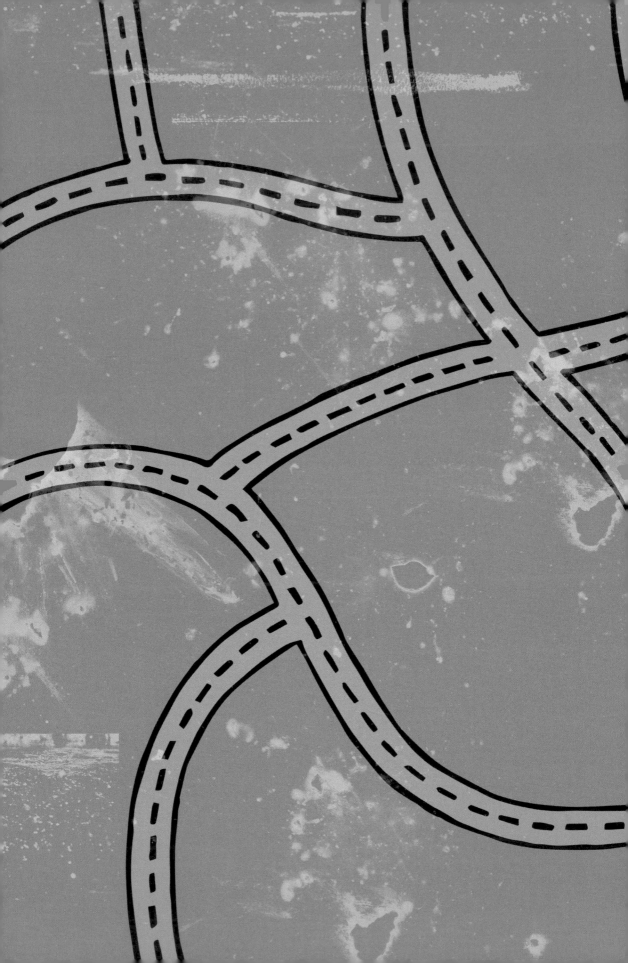